THIS BOOK BELONGS TO

START DATE

| MONTH | DAY | YEAR |

EDITORIAL

EDITORS-IN-CHIEF
Raechel Myers & Amanda Bible Williams

CONTENT DIRECTOR
Russ Ramsey, MDiv., ThM.

MANAGING EDITOR
Jessica Lamb

EDITOR
Kara Gause

EDITORIAL ASSISTANT
Ellen Taylor

CREATIVE

CREATIVE DIRECTOR
Ryan Myers

ART DIRECTOR
Amanda Barnhart

DESIGNER
Kelsea Allen

PRODUCTION DESIGNER
Julie Allen

LETTERER
Emily Knapp

PHOTOGRAPHERS
Katherine Huskey (29, 33, 55, 73, 83)
Jordana Nicholson (41, 59)

SHE READS TRUTH™

© 2018 by She Reads Truth, LLC

ISBN 978-1-946282-62-0

All Scripture is taken from the Christian Standard Bible®, Copyright © 2017 by Holman Bible Publishers. Used by permission. Christian Standard Bible® and CSB® are federally registered trademarks of Holman Bible Publishers.

Though the dates in this book have been carefully researched, scholars disagree on the dating of many biblical events.

@SHEREADSTRUTH

SHEREADSTRUTH.COM

SUBSCRIPTION INQUIRIES
orders@shereadstruth.com

This book was printed offset in Nashville, Tennessee, on Neenah Classic Textures Avalanche White, Stipple 100C with a clear gloss UV.

PSALMS FOR PRAYER

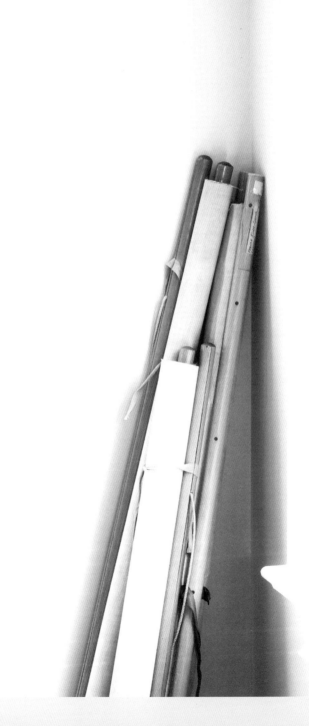

Prayer is a startling invitation—one that, after 30 years of following Jesus, I still struggle to accept.

"Call to me and I will answer you and tell you great and incomprehensible things you do not know," the Lord says to His people in Jeremiah 33:3. The book of Hebrews urges the Christ follower to "approach the throne of grace with boldness" (4:16), and Paul tells the Philippians not to worry about anything, but instead to petition God in prayer (4:6). Perhaps most astonishing of all, Jesus Himself instructs His disciples, "Whenever you pray, say, Father..." (Lk 11:2).

Call out to God. Go boldly to the throne. Ask instead of worry. Talk to God as your Father.

This is the invitation. But what do we say? How do we find the words to pray?

Prayer, like everything else in the Christian life, is a practice learned over time. When it comes to learning the language of prayer, there is no better classroom than the Psalms. The book of Psalms was the hymn and prayer book for the people of God before the days of Jesus. God's people have been praying these writings, and using them to shape their own prayers, ever since.

In this *Psalms for Prayer* study book, we've selected fifteen psalms for you to use when you pray. They cover a range of topics, from glorifying God, to praying for our personal concerns, to lifting up the needs of this world. Some of these psalms are worded as prayers offered directly to God; others act as prompts to inspire prayer. At the end of each reading, you'll find interactive elements designed to help you practice the art of prayer: a worksheet for studying the day's psalm, and a page for writing your own prayer in response.

Three decades after my first prayer, I'm still learning how to talk to God. I'm a person accustomed to communicating with other people, after all, and prayer is wholly other. There is no hiding, no putting on airs, no manipulation. All attempts at deceit are futile. God created us with the capacity to feel the very emotions we try to conceal. He knows our needs before we ask (Mt 6:8), and our every circumstance exists in the context of His kingdom. There is nothing—not even our hearts—over which He does not rule.

May God use your time in these psalms to reveal more of His character and love to you. May He draw you into a daily and ongoing conversation with Him, and may His Word teach you to express your heart to Him in prayer.

Your fellow student,

Amanda

Amanda Bible Williams
EDITOR-IN-CHIEF

> CALL OUT TO GOD.
> GO BOLDLY TO THE
> THRONE. ASK INSTEAD
> OF WORRY. TALK TO
> GOD AS YOUR FATHER.

"

THE THICK, DRY MARKER STYLE
COMMUNICATES THE REALITY
OF OUR NEED FOR GOD AND
THE RAWNESS OF SHARING OUR
MOST PRIVATE THOUGHTS AND
FEELINGS IN PRAYER.

Prayer is an intimate experience between the believer and God. We wanted the design of this book to reflect that in every detail, from color selection to paper stock. We chose a stipple cover with a subtle pebble finish to give this book of prayers a unique, tactile touch.

To create an atmosphere of stillness on a two-dimensional page, we committed to restraint in design by leaning heavily on the use of white space. Color is leveraged in only a few places, most noticeably in the "Emotion in the Psalms" chart on page 88. We also curated a selection of photographs with minimal subject matter to symbolize a place of contemplation.

Our in-house letterer used a dry brush technique throughout the book to further represent the emotion in these psalms. The thick, dry marker style communicates the reality of our need for God and the rawness of sharing our most private thoughts and feelings in prayer. Because we enjoyed working with this technique ourselves, we included a lettering activity on page 108 for you to practice this style.

May the aesthetic beauty of this book further point you to the inherent beauty of God's love for you.

THE SHE READS TRUTH CREATIVE TEAM

She Reads Truth is a community of women dedicated to reading the Word of God every day.

The Bible is living and active, breathed out by God, and we confidently hold it higher than anything we can do or say. Designed for a Monday start, this book focuses primarily on Scripture, with bonus resources to facilitate deeper engagement with God's Word.

SCRIPTURE READING

This study book presents a series of psalms for prayer in daily readings. Each weekday features an interactive worksheet for studying the day's psalm.

A worksheet example is included on page 25.

PRAYER

Each weekday also features space for writing your own prayer.

GRACE DAY

Use Saturdays to pray, rest, and reflect on what you've read.

For added community and conversation, join us in the **Psalms for Prayer** reading plan on the She Reads Truth app or at SheReadsTruth.com.

WEEKLY TRUTH

Sundays are set aside for weekly Scripture memorization.

Find the corresponding memory cards in the back of your book.

EXTRAS

"WHEN YOU PRAY TO GOD IN PSALMS AND HYMNS, THINK OVER IN YOUR HEARTS THE WORDS THAT COME FROM YOUR LIPS."

Augustine

ELEMENTS OF PRAYER IN THE PSALMS

While prayer appears in the Bible in a variety of formats, almost every instance includes the five elements listed here. The pages that follow provide examples of each element from the psalms in this reading plan. Refer back to this guide as you write your own prayers.

ADDRESS. DESCRIBE. CONFESS. REQUEST. PRAISE.

1	2	3	4	5
How God is addressed	Details describing the situation	Confession of sin and need	Appeals for help	Words of thanks and adoration to God

ADDRESS

HOW GOD IS ADDRESSED

"God, the one enthroned from long ago..." PS 55:19

"...the Maker of heaven and earth, the sea and everything in them..." PS 146:6

"You are my shelter, my portion in the land of the living." PS 142:5

"The LORD is my shepherd." PS 23:1

"The LORD is my light and my salvation..." PS 27:1

DESCRIBE

2

DETAILS DESCRIBING THE SITUATION

"My friend acts violently against those at peace with him; he violates his covenant." PS 55:20

"...the nations rage and the people plot in vain." PS 2:1

"I am weary from my groaning; with my tears I dampen my bed..." PS 6:6

"For the enemy has pursued me, crushing me to the ground..." PS 143:3

"My hands were continually lifted up all night long; I refused to be comforted." PS 77:2

CONFESS

3

CONFESSION OF SIN AND NEED

"I was guilty when I was born; I was sinful when my mother conceived me." PS 51:5

"Don't hide your face from me, or I will be like those going down to the Pit." PS 143:7

"I am weak; heal me, LORD, for my bones are shaking." PS 6:2

"Against you—you alone—I have sinned and done this evil in your sight." PS 51:4

"I am poor and needy." PS 86:1

REQUEST

4

APPEALS FOR HELP

"Rescue me from those who pursue me…" PS 142:6

"Reveal to me the way I should go…" PS 143:8

"Restore the joy of your salvation to me, and sustain me by giving me a willing spirit." PS 51:12

"Bring joy to your servant's life…" PS 86:4

"Lord, hear my voice when I call." PS 27:7

PRAISE

5

WORDS OF THANKS AND
ADORATION TO GOD

"I will sing to my God as long as I live..." PS 146:2

"Happy is the person who trusts in you, LORD of Armies!"
PS 84:12

"For your faithful love for me is great..." PS 86:13

"...your decrees are my delight and my counselors."
PS 119:24

"How countless are your works, LORD! In wisdom you have
made them all." PS 104:24

"WE MUST LAY BEFORE HIM WHAT IS IN US,
NOT WHAT OUGHT TO BE IN US."

C. S. Lewis

ON THE TIMELINE

The book of Psalms consists of many different hymns and prayers. Taking the names in the titles as authors, the date of composition ranges from the time of Moses (fifteenth century BC) to a time following the Exile (sixth century BC or later). Some of the titles contain historical information that might indicate the setting of the psalm, although even this, like authorship, is subject to interpretation.

A LITTLE BACKGROUND

Since the book of Psalms contains a variety of psalms written over a long period of time, there is no one author for the collection. By far the most common designation in the titles is "of David," which likely refers to King David. David's role as a musician in Saul's court (1Sm 16:14-23), as well as his experience as a shepherd, soldier, and king, make him a likely candidate for writing many of the psalms. Other titles include the designations of Solomon (Ps 72; 127), Asaph (Ps 50; 73-83), the sons of Korah (Ps 42; 44-49; 84-85; 87-88), Ethan (Ps 89), and Moses (Ps 90).

MESSAGE & PURPOSE

The full range of human emotions is shown in the Psalms. This record of the responses of God's people in worship and prayer serves the purpose of teaching us how to relate to God in various circumstances of life. The Psalms also demonstrate God's sovereignty and goodness to His people in order to instill confidence in those who trust in Him.

GIVE THANKS FOR THE BOOK OF PSALMS

The Psalms are deeply relational. They give us a window into who God is, how He acts, and how His people respond. The struggle to understand how God's attributes, particularly His sovereignty and goodness, relate to life experiences is a major theme throughout the Psalms. These words are from people who had not lost their faith in God, although they might have been tempted to at times (Ps 73). Like us, they wrestled with how God was dealing with them personally and as a community.

LORD, HEAR MY VOICE WHEN I CALL;
BE GRACIOUS TO ME AND ANSWER ME.
MY HEART SAYS THIS ABOUT YOU:
"SEEK HIS FACE."
LORD, I WILL SEEK YOUR FACE.

KEY VERSE | PSALM 27:7-8

A PRAYER FOR DELIVERANCE

PSALM

Each weekday features a psalm, a worksheet for studying the psalm, and space for writing a prayer in response. We've completed this worksheet example, using Psalm 54, for you to refer back to as needed.

For the choir director: with stringed instruments. A Maskil of David. When the Ziphites went and said to Saul, "Is David not hiding among us?"

1 God, save me by your name,
   and vindicate me by your might!
2 God, hear my prayer;
   listen to the words from my mouth.
3 For strangers rise up against me,
   and violent men intend to kill me.
   They do not let God guide them.   *Selah*

4 God is my helper;
   the Lord is the sustainer of my life.
5 He will repay my adversaries for their evil.
   Because of your faithfulness,
      annihilate them.

6 I will sacrifice a freewill offering to you.
   I will praise your name, LORD,
   because it is good.
7 For he has rescued me from every trouble,
   and my eye has looked down on my enemies.

AUTHOR   ASAPH   ✗ DAVID   SONS OF KORAH   UNSPECIFIED

What emotions are present in this psalm?

✗ ANGER

✗ ANXIETY

☐ DELIGHT

☐ FEAR

✗ GRATITUDE

✗ GRIEF

☐ HOPE

✗ JOY

☐ LONGING

☐ LOVE

✗ OPTIMISM

☐ PEACE

☐ REMORSE

☐ SORROW

☐ SYMPATHY

✗ OTHER

Adoration

For more options, see the "Emotion in the Psalms" chart on p. 88.

What does the psalm say about the psalmist's circumstance?

- Strangers rise up against me
- Violent men intend to kill me

How does the psalmist describe himself?

- In trouble
- In hiding
- Surrounded
- Devoted to God

What requests are made to God?

- Hear my prayer
- Listen to the words of my mouth
- Vindicate me

What instructions are given to the reader?

- It is good to praise the name of the Lord

How is God addressed and/or described?

- My Helper
- Sustainer of my life
- Lord
- He has rescued me from every trouble

What situation in my life does this psalm call to mind?

- Someone is slandering my character. I don't know what to do.

A PRAYER PRAISING GOD'S GREATNESS

PSALM

A hymn of David.

1 I exalt you, my God the King,
and bless your name forever and ever.
2 I will bless you every day;
I will praise your name forever and ever.

3 The LORD is great and is highly praised;
his greatness is unsearchable.
4 One generation will declare your works
to the next
and will proclaim your mighty acts.
5 I will speak of your splendor and glorious majesty
and your wondrous works.
6 They will proclaim the power of your
awe-inspiring acts,
and I will declare your greatness.
7 They will give a testimony of your great goodness
and will joyfully sing of your righteousness.

8 The LORD is gracious and compassionate,
slow to anger and great in faithful love.
9 The LORD is good to everyone;
his compassion rests on all he has made.
10 All you have made will thank you, LORD;
the faithful will bless you.
11 They will speak of the glory of your kingdom
and will declare your might,

12 informing all people of your mighty acts
and of the glorious splendor of your kingdom.
13 Your kingdom is an everlasting kingdom;
your rule is for all generations.
The LORD is faithful in all his words
and gracious in all his actions.

14 The LORD helps all who fall;
he raises up all who are oppressed.
15 All eyes look to you,
and you give them their food at the proper time.
16 You open your hand
and satisfy the desire of every living thing.

17 The LORD is righteous in all his ways
and faithful in all his acts.
18 The LORD is near all who call out to him,
all who call out to him with integrity.
19 He fulfills the desires of those who fear him;
he hears their cry for help and saves them.
20 The LORD guards all those who love him,
but he destroys all the wicked.
21 My mouth will declare the LORD's praise;
let every living thing
bless his holy name forever and ever.

Use the worksheet below to study Psalm 145, and use the following page to write your own prayer based on what you learn.

PSALM 145

AUTHOR ☐ ASAPH ☐ DAVID ☐ SONS OF KORAH ☐ UNSPECIFIED

What emotions are present in this psalm?

What does the psalm say about the psalmist's circumstance?

☐ ANGER

☐ ANXIETY

☐ DELIGHT

☐ FEAR

How does the psalmist describe himself?

☐ GRATITUDE

☐ GRIEF

☐ HOPE

☐ JOY

What requests are made to God?

What instructions are given to the reader?

How is God addressed and/or described?

☐ LONGING

☐ LOVE

☐ OPTIMISM

☐ PEACE

☐ REMORSE

☐ SORROW

☐ SYMPATHY

☐ OTHER

_____

For more options, see the "Emotion in the Psalms" chart on p. 88.

What situation in my life does this psalm call to mind?

© 2018 She Reads Truth. All rights reserved.

SHE READS TRUTH 27

Write your own prayer below, using the "Elements of Prayer in the Psalms" guide on pp.11-21 as a reference.

ADDRESS. DESCRIBE. CONFESS. REQUEST. PRAISE.

THE LORD IS FAITHFUL IN ALL HIS WORDS
AND GRACIOUS IN ALL HIS ACTIONS.

PSALM 145:13

A PRAYER CELEBRATING GOD'S CREATION

PSALM

1 My soul, bless the LORD!
LORD my God, you are very great;
you are clothed with majesty and
splendor.
2 He wraps himself in light as if it were
a robe,
spreading out the sky like a canopy,
3 laying the beams of his palace
on the waters above,
making the clouds his chariot,
walking on the wings of the wind,
4 and making the winds his messengers,
flames of fire his servants.

5 He established the earth on its
foundations;
it will never be shaken.
6 You covered it with the deep
as if it were a garment;
the water stood above the mountains.
7 At your rebuke the water fled;
at the sound of your thunder they
hurried away—
8 mountains rose and valleys sank—
to the place you established for them.
9 You set a boundary they cannot cross;
they will never cover the earth again.

10 He causes the springs to gush into the
valleys;
they flow between the mountains.
11 They supply water for every wild beast;
the wild donkeys quench their thirst.

12 The birds of the sky live beside the
springs;
they make their voices heard among
the foliage.
13 He waters the mountains from his
palace;
the earth is satisfied by the fruit of
your labor.

14 He causes grass to grow for the
livestock
and provides crops for man to
cultivate,
producing food from the earth,
15 wine that makes human hearts glad—
making his face shine with oil—
and bread that sustains human hearts.

16 The trees of the LORD flourish,
the cedars of Lebanon that he planted.
17 here the birds make their nests;
storks make their homes in the pine
trees.
18 The high mountains are for the wild
goats;
the cliffs are a refuge for hyraxes.

19 He made the moon to mark the
festivals;
the sun knows when to set.
20 You bring darkness, and it becomes
night,
when all the forest animals stir.
21 The young lions roar for their prey
and seek their food from God.
22 The sun rises; they go back
and lie down in their dens.
23 Man goes out to his work
and to his labor until evening.

24 How countless are your works, LORD!
In wisdom you have made them all;
the earth is full of your creatures.
25 Here is the sea, vast and wide,
teeming with creatures beyond
number—
living things both large and small.
26 There the ships move about,
and Leviathan, which you formed to
play there.

27 All of them wait for you
to give them their food at the right time.
28 When you give it to them,
they gather it;
when you open your hand,
they are satisfied with good things.
29 When you hide your face,
they are terrified;
when you take away their breath,
they die and return to the dust.
30 When you send your breath,
they are created,
and you renew the surface of the ground.

31 May the glory of the LORD endure
forever;
may the LORD rejoice in his works.
32 He looks at the earth, and it trembles;
he touches the mountains,
and they pour out smoke.
33 I will sing to the LORD all my life;
I will sing praise to my God while I live.
34 May my meditation be pleasing to him;
I will rejoice in the LORD.
35 May sinners vanish from the earth
and wicked people be no more.
My soul, bless the LORD!
Hallelujah!

AUTHOR   ☐ ASAPH   ☐ DAVID   ☐ SONS OF KORAH   ☐ UNSPECIFIED

What emotions are present in this psalm?

☐ ANGER

☐ ANXIETY

☐ DELIGHT

☐ FEAR

☐ GRATITUDE

☐ GRIEF

☐ HOPE

☐ JOY

☐ LONGING

☐ LOVE

☐ OPTIMISM

☐ PEACE

☐ REMORSE

☐ SORROW

☐ SYMPATHY

☐ OTHER

_____

For more options, see the "Emotion in the Psalms" chart on p. 88.

What does the psalm say about the psalmist's circumstance?

How does the psalmist describe himself?

What requests are made to God?	What instructions are given to the reader?	How is God addressed and/or described?

What situation in my life does this psalm call to mind?

Write your own prayer below.

ADDRESS. DESCRIBE. CONFESS. REQUEST. PRAISE.

HOW COUNTLESS ARE YOUR WORKS, LORD!

PSALM 104:24

A PRAYER FOR WHEN GOD SEEMS SILENT

PSALM

For the choir director: according to Jeduthun. Of Asaph. A psalm.

1 I cry aloud to God,
aloud to God, and he will hear me.
2 I sought the Lord in my day of trouble.
My hands were continually lifted up
all night long;
I refused to be comforted.
3 I think of God; I groan;
I meditate; my spirit becomes weak. *Selah*

4 You have kept me from closing my eyes;
I am troubled and cannot speak.
5 I consider days of old,
years long past.
6 At night I remember my music;
I meditate in my heart, and my spirit ponders.

7 "Will the Lord reject forever
and never again show favor?
8 Has his faithful love ceased forever?
Is his promise at an end for all generations?
9 Has God forgotten to be gracious?
Has he in anger withheld his compassion?" *Selah*

10 So I say, "I am grieved
that the right hand of the Most High
has changed."

11 I will remember the LORD's works;
yes, I will remember your ancient wonders.
12 I will reflect on all you have done
and meditate on your actions.

13 God, your way is holy.
What god is great like God?
14 You are the God who works wonders;
you revealed your strength among the peoples.
15 With power you redeemed your people,
the descendants of Jacob and Joseph. *Selah*

16 The water saw you, God.
The water saw you; it trembled.
Even the depths shook.
17 The clouds poured down water.
The storm clouds thundered;
your arrows flashed back and forth.
18 The sound of your thunder was in
the whirlwind;
lightning lit up the world.
The earth shook and quaked.
19 Your way went through the sea
and your path through the vast water,
but your footprints were unseen.
20 You led your people like a flock
by the hand of Moses and Aaron.

AUTHOR ☐ ASAPH ☐ DAVID ☐ SONS OF KORAH ☐ UNSPECIFIED

What emotions are present in this psalm?

What does the psalm say about the psalmist's circumstance?

☐ ANGER

☐ ANXIETY

☐ DELIGHT

How does the psalmist describe himself?

☐ FEAR

☐ GRATITUDE

☐ GRIEF

☐ HOPE

☐ JOY

What requests are made to God?	What instructions are given to the reader?	How is God addressed and/or described?

☐ LONGING

☐ LOVE

☐ OPTIMISM

☐ PEACE

☐ REMORSE

☐ SORROW

☐ SYMPATHY

☐ OTHER

For more options, see the "Emotion in the Psalms" chart on p. 88.

What situation in my life does this psalm call to mind?

Write your own prayer below.

ADDRESS. DESCRIBE. CONFESS. REQUEST. PRAISE.

YOU ARE THE GOD WHO
WORKS WONDERS.

PSALM 77:14

A PRAYER CELEBRATING GOD'S WORD

PSALM

vv. 1-32

א *Aleph*

1 How happy are those whose way
    is blameless,
  who walk according to the LORD's
    instruction!
2 Happy are those who keep his decrees
  and seek him with all their heart.
3 They do nothing wrong;
  they walk in his ways.
4 You have commanded that
    your precepts
  be diligently kept.
5 If only my ways were committed
  to keeping your statutes!
6 Then I would not be ashamed
  when I think about all your
    commands.
7 I will praise you with an upright heart
  when I learn your righteous
    judgments.
8 I will keep your statutes;
  never abandon me.

ב *Beth*

9 How can a young man keep his
    way pure?
  By keeping your word.
10 I have sought you with all my heart;
  don't let me wander from your
    commands.
11 I have treasured your word in
    my heart
  so that I may not sin against you.

12 LORD, may you be blessed;
  teach me your statutes.
13 With my lips I proclaim
  all the judgments from your mouth.
14 I rejoice in the way revealed by
    your decrees
  as much as in all riches.
15 I will meditate on your precepts
  and think about your ways.
16 I will delight in your statutes;
  I will not forget your word.

ג *Gimel*

17 Deal generously with your servant
  so that I might live;
  then I will keep your word.
18 Open my eyes so that I may
    contemplate
  wondrous things from your
    instruction.
19 I am a resident alien on earth;
  do not hide your commands from me.
20 I am continually overcome
  with longing for your judgments.
21 You rebuke the arrogant,
  the ones under a curse,
  who wander from your commands.
22 Take insult and contempt away
    from me,
  for I have kept your decrees.
23 Though princes sit together speaking
    against me,

  your servant will think about
    your statutes;
24 your decrees are my delight
  and my counselors.

ד *Daleth*

25 My life is down in the dust;
  give me life through your word.
26 I told you about my life,
  and you answered me;
  teach me your statutes.
27 Help me understand
  the meaning of your precepts
  so that I can meditate on
    your wonders.
28 I am weary from grief;
  strengthen me through your word.
29 Keep me from the way of deceit
  and graciously give me
    your instruction.
30 I have chosen the way of truth;
  I have set your ordinances before me.
31 I cling to your decrees;
  LORD, do not put me to shame.
32 I pursue the way of your commands,
  for you broaden my understanding.

AUTHOR   ☐ ASAPH   ☐ DAVID   ☐ SONS OF KORAH   ☐ UNSPECIFIED

What emotions are present in this psalm?

☐ ANGER

☐ ANXIETY

☐ DELIGHT

☐ FEAR

☐ GRATITUDE

☐ GRIEF

☐ HOPE

☐ JOY

☐ LONGING

☐ LOVE

☐ OPTIMISM

☐ PEACE

☐ REMORSE

☐ SORROW

☐ SYMPATHY

☐ OTHER

_____

For more options, see the "Emotion in the Psalms" chart on p. 88.

What does the psalm say about the psalmist's circumstance?

How does the psalmist describe himself?

What requests are made to God?	What instructions are given to the reader?	How is God addressed and/or described?

What situation in my life does this psalm call to mind?

Write your own prayer below.

ADDRESS. DESCRIBE. CONFESS. REQUEST. PRAISE.

I HAVE TREASURED YOUR WORD IN MY HEART
SO THAT I MAY NOT SIN AGAINST YOU.

PSALM 119:11

A PRAYER WHEN BATTLING ANXIETY

PSALM

Of David.

1 The Lord is my light and my salvation—
whom should I fear?
The Lord is the stronghold of my life—
whom should I dread?
2 When evildoers came against me to devour
my flesh,
my foes and my enemies stumbled and fell.
3 Though an army deploys against me,
my heart will not be afraid;
though a war breaks out against me,
I will still be confident.

4 I have asked one thing from the Lord;
it is what I desire:
to dwell in the house of the Lord
all the days of my life,
gazing on the beauty of the Lord
and seeking him in his temple.
5 For he will conceal me in his shelter
in the day of adversity;
he will hide me under the cover of his tent;
he will set me high on a rock.
6 Then my head will be high
above my enemies around me;
I will offer sacrifices in his tent with shouts of joy.
I will sing and make music to the Lord.

7 Lord, hear my voice when I call;
be gracious to me and answer me.
8 My heart says this about you:
"Seek his face."
Lord, I will seek your face.
9 Do not hide your face from me;
do not turn your servant away in anger.
You have been my helper;
do not leave me or abandon me,
God of my salvation.
10 Even if my father and mother abandon me,
the Lord cares for me.

11 Because of my adversaries,
show me your way, Lord,
and lead me on a level path.
12 Do not give me over to the will of my foes,
for false witnesses rise up against me,
breathing violence.

13 I am certain that I will see the Lord's goodness
in the land of the living.
14 Wait for the Lord;
be strong, and let your heart be courageous.
Wait for the Lord.

AUTHOR   ☐ ASAPH   ☐ DAVID   ☐ SONS OF KORAH   ☐ UNSPECIFIED

What emotions are
present in this psalm?

What does the psalm say about the psalmist's circumstance?

☐ ANGER

☐ ANXIETY

☐ DELIGHT

How does the psalmist describe himself?

☐ FEAR

☐ GRATITUDE

☐ GRIEF

☐ HOPE

☐ JOY

What requests are made to God?

What instructions are given to
the reader?

How is God addressed
and/or described?

☐ LONGING

☐ LOVE

☐ OPTIMISM

☐ PEACE

☐ REMORSE

☐ SORROW

☐ SYMPATHY

☐ OTHER

*For more options, see the "Emotion
in the Psalms" chart on p. 88.*

What situation in my life does this psalm call to mind?

Write your own prayer below.

ADDRESS. DESCRIBE. CONFESS. REQUEST. PRAISE.

I AM CERTAIN THAT I WILL SEE THE LORD'S
GOODNESS IN THE LAND OF THE LIVING.

PSALM 27:13

Use today to pray, rest, and reflect
on this week's reading, giving thanks
for the grace that is ours in Christ.

HE SAID TO THEM,
"WHENEVER YOU PRAY, SAY,

FATHER,
YOUR NAME BE HONORED AS HOLY.
YOUR KINGDOM COME.
GIVE US EACH DAY OUR DAILY BREAD.
AND FORGIVE US OUR SINS,
FOR WE OURSELVES ALSO FORGIVE
EVERYONE IN DEBT TO US.
AND DO NOT BRING US INTO TEMPTATION."

LUKE 11:2-4

GRACE DAY

Scripture is God-breathed and true. When we memorize it, we carry the gospel with us wherever we go.

This week we will memorize the key verse for this reading plan.

Find the corresponding memory card in the back of your book.

LORD, HEAR MY VOICE WHEN I CALL;
BE GRACIOUS TO ME AND ANSWER ME.
MY HEART SAYS THIS ABOUT YOU:
"SEEK HIS FACE."
LORD, I WILL SEEK YOUR FACE.

PSALM 27:7-8

WEEKLY TRUTH

"Christian character grows in the secret place of prayer."

SAMUEL M. ZWEMER

A PRAYER IN TIMES OF SORROW

PSALM

A prayer of David.

1 Listen, LORD, and answer me,
   for I am poor and needy.
2 Protect my life, for I am faithful.
   You are my God; save your servant who
      trusts in you.
3 Be gracious to me, Lord,
   for I call to you all day long.
4 Bring joy to your servant's life,
   because I appeal to you, Lord.

5 For you, Lord, are kind and ready to forgive,
   abounding in faithful love to all who
      call on you.
6 LORD, hear my prayer;
   listen to my plea for mercy.
7 I call on you in the day of my distress,
   for you will answer me.

8 Lord, there is no one like you among the gods,
   and there are no works like yours.
9 All the nations you have made
   will come and bow down before you, Lord,
   and will honor your name.
10 For you are great and perform wonders;
   you alone are God.

11 Teach me your way, LORD,
   and I will live by your truth.
   Give me an undivided mind to fear your name.
12 I will praise you with all my heart,
      Lord my God,
   and will honor your name forever.
13 For your faithful love for me is great,
   and you rescue my life from the depths
      of Sheol.

14 God, arrogant people have attacked me;
   a gang of ruthless men intends to kill me.
   They do not let you guide them.
15 But you, Lord, are a compassionate and
      gracious God,
   slow to anger and abounding in faithful
      love and truth.
16 Turn to me and be gracious to me.
   Give your strength to your servant;
   save the son of your female servant.
17 Show me a sign of your goodness;
   my enemies will see and be put to shame
   because you, LORD, have helped and
      comforted me.

AUTHOR   ☐ ASAPH   ☐ DAVID   ☐ SONS OF KORAH   ☐ UNSPECIFIED

What emotions are present in this psalm?

What does the psalm say about the psalmist's circumstance?

☐ ANGER

☐ ANXIETY

☐ DELIGHT

☐ FEAR

How does the psalmist describe himself?

☐ GRATITUDE

☐ GRIEF

☐ HOPE

☐ JOY

What requests are made to God?	What instructions are given to the reader?	How is God addressed and/or described?

☐ LONGING

☐ LOVE

☐ OPTIMISM

☐ PEACE

☐ REMORSE

☐ SORROW

☐ SYMPATHY

☐ OTHER

_____

For more options, see the "Emotion in the Psalms" chart on p. 88.

What situation in my life does this psalm call to mind?

Write your own prayer below.

ADDRESS. DESCRIBE. CONFESS. REQUEST. PRAISE.

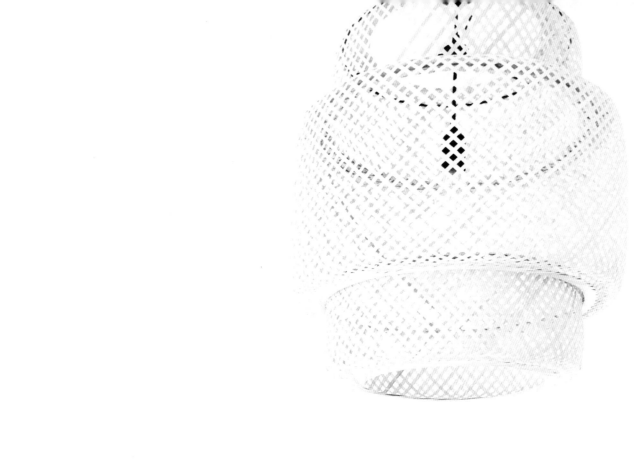

I WILL PRAISE YOU WITH
ALL MY HEART, LORD MY
GOD, AND WILL HONOR
YOUR NAME FOREVER.

PSALM 86:12

A PRAYER FOR MERCY

PSALM

For the choir director: with stringed instruments,
according to Sheminith. A psalm of David.

1   Lord, do not rebuke me in your anger;
    do not discipline me in your wrath.
2   Be gracious to me, Lord, for I am weak;
    heal me, Lord, for my bones are shaking;
3   my whole being is shaken with terror.
    And you, Lord—how long?

4   Turn, Lord! Rescue me;
    save me because of your faithful love.
5   For there is no remembrance of you in death;
    who can thank you in Sheol?

6   I am weary from my groaning;
    with my tears I dampen my bed
    and drench my couch every night.
7   My eyes are swollen from grief;
    they grow old because of all my enemies.

8   Depart from me, all evildoers,
    for the Lord has heard the sound
      of my weeping.
9   The Lord has heard my plea for help;
    the Lord accepts my prayer.
10 All my enemies will be ashamed and shake
      with terror;
    they will turn back and suddenly be disgraced.

AUTHOR ☐ ASAPH ☐ DAVID ☐ SONS OF KORAH ☐ UNSPECIFIED

What emotions are present in this psalm?

What does the psalm say about the psalmist's circumstance?

☐ ANGER

☐ ANXIETY

☐ DELIGHT

How does the psalmist describe himself?

☐ FEAR

☐ GRATITUDE

☐ GRIEF

☐ HOPE

☐ JOY

☐ LONGING

☐ LOVE

☐ OPTIMISM

☐ PEACE

☐ REMORSE

☐ SORROW

☐ SYMPATHY

☐ OTHER

For more options, see the "Emotion in the Psalms" chart on p. 88.

What requests are made to God?	What instructions are given to the reader?	How is God addressed and/or described?

What situation in my life does this psalm call to mind?

Write your own prayer below.

ADDRESS. DESCRIBE. CONFESS. REQUEST. PRAISE.

THE LORD HAS HEARD MY PLEA FOR HELP;
THE LORD ACCEPTS MY PRAYER.

PSALM 6:9

How should we pray? What should we keep in mind as we do? Practicing the art of prayer is one of the great rewards of following Jesus over the course of time. Here are some reminders and tips to help.

Remember

With God, all things are possible.	MARK 10:27
Jesus is our Great High Priest who is always interceding for us.	HEBREWS 7:24-25
The Holy Spirit lives in the hearts of all believers.	1 CORINTHIANS 3:16
God sees things perfectly, even when we can't. Our personal feelings do not dictate what is actually true.	EPHESIANS 1:17-19
Prayer should be honest. God already knows our hearts.	ACTS 15:8
God is merciful and kind.	PSALM 145:8
God has already proven the depth of His love for us by giving us His Son.	JOHN 3:16
Prayer requires faith.	MATTHEW 21:22
Prayer is a form of worship.	PSALM 29:1-2
Prayer isn't meant to be a performance.	MATTHEW 6:5-6
Prayer is meant to change us.	PSALM 119:26-27

Practice

Read Scripture when you pray. It is God's Word to us.	ROMANS 10:17
Pray in Jesus' name, acknowledging that He is the only way we can approach God.	JOHN 14:6
Ask for the Holy Spirit's help.	ROMANS 8:26-27
Revere God's name, and use Scripture to expand your vocabulary in terms of how you address Him.	MATTHEW 6:9 ISAIAH 9:6
Ask God to help you examine your own heart as you pray.	PSALM 26:2
Practice confessing sin and accepting forgiveness.	LUKE 18:13
Plan. Set aside time for prayer and Scripture reading.	MARK 1:35
Pray spontaneous, simple prayers throughout the day.	1 THESSALONIANS 5:17-18
Ask God for what you need, and be willing to ask more than once.	MATTHEW 7:9-11 LUKE 18:4-8
Pray for others, not just yourself.	PHILIPPIANS 2:3-4
Give thanks to God.	PHILIPPIANS 4:6

A PRAYER FOR COMFORT

PSALM

A psalm of David.

1 The LORD is my shepherd;
I have what I need.
2 He lets me lie down in green pastures;
he leads me beside quiet waters.
3 He renews my life;
he leads me along the right paths
for his name's sake.
4 Even when I go through the darkest valley,
I fear no danger,
for you are with me;
your rod and your staff—they comfort me.

5 You prepare a table before me
in the presence of my enemies;
you anoint my head with oil;
my cup overflows.
6 Only goodness and faithful love will pursue me
all the days of my life,
and I will dwell in the house of the LORD
as long as I live.

AUTHOR ☐ ASAPH ☐ DAVID ☐ SONS OF KORAH ☐ UNSPECIFIED

What emotions are present in this psalm?

What does the psalm say about the psalmist's circumstance?

☐ ANGER

☐ ANXIETY

☐ DELIGHT

How does the psalmist describe himself?

☐ FEAR

☐ GRATITUDE

☐ GRIEF

☐ HOPE

☐ JOY

What requests are made to God?

☐ LONGING

☐ LOVE

☐ OPTIMISM

☐ PEACE

☐ REMORSE

☐ SORROW

☐ SYMPATHY

☐ OTHER

What instructions are given to the reader?

How is God addressed and/or described?

For more options, see the "Emotion in the Psalms" chart on p. 88.

What situation in my life does this psalm call to mind?

Write your own prayer below.

ADDRESS. DESCRIBE. CONFESS. REQUEST. PRAISE.

HE LETS ME LIE DOWN IN GREEN PASTURES;
HE LEADS ME BESIDE QUIET WATERS.

PSALM 23:2

A PRAYER FOR FORGIVENESS

PSALM

For the choir director. A psalm of David, when the prophet Nathan came to him after he had gone to Bathsheba.

1 Be gracious to me, God,
according to your faithful love;
according to your abundant compassion,
blot out my rebellion.
2 Completely wash away my guilt
and cleanse me from my sin.
3 For I am conscious of my rebellion,
and my sin is always before me.
4 Against you—you alone—I have sinned
and done this evil in your sight.
So you are right when you pass sentence;
you are blameless when you judge.
5 Indeed, I was guilty when I was born;
I was sinful when my mother conceived me.

6 Surely you desire integrity in the inner self,
and you teach me wisdom deep within.
7 Purify me with hyssop, and I will be clean;
wash me, and I will be whiter than snow.
8 Let me hear joy and gladness;
let the bones you have crushed rejoice.
9 Turn your face away from my sins
and blot out all my guilt.

10 God, create a clean heart for me
and renew a steadfast spirit within me.
11 Do not banish me from your presence
or take your Holy Spirit from me.
12 Restore the joy of your salvation to me,
and sustain me by giving me a willing spirit.
13 Then I will teach the rebellious your ways,
and sinners will return to you.

14 Save me from the guilt of bloodshed, God—
God of my salvation—
and my tongue will sing of your righteousness.
15 Lord, open my lips,
and my mouth will declare your praise.
16 You do not want a sacrifice, or I would give it;
you are not pleased with a burnt offering.
17 The sacrifice pleasing to God is a broken spirit.
You will not despise a broken and humbled
heart, God.

18 In your good pleasure, cause Zion to prosper;
build the walls of Jerusalem.
19 Then you will delight in righteous sacrifices,
whole burnt offerings;
then bulls will be offered on your altar.

AUTHOR ☐ ASAPH ☐ DAVID ☐ SONS OF KORAH ☐ UNSPECIFIED

What emotions are
present in this psalm?

What does the psalm say about the psalmist's circumstance?

☐ ANGER

☐ ANXIETY

☐ DELIGHT

How does the psalmist describe himself?

☐ FEAR

☐ GRATITUDE

☐ GRIEF

☐ HOPE

☐ JOY

What requests are made to God?	What instructions are given to the reader?	How is God addressed and/or described?

☐ LONGING

☐ LOVE

☐ OPTIMISM

☐ PEACE

☐ REMORSE

☐ SORROW

☐ SYMPATHY

☐ OTHER

For more options, see the "Emotion in the Psalms" chart on p. 88.

What situation in my life does this psalm call to mind?

Write your own prayer below.

ADDRESS. DESCRIBE. CONFESS. REQUEST. PRAISE.

THE SACRIFICE PLEASING TO GOD
IS A BROKEN SPIRIT.
YOU WILL NOT DESPISE A BROKEN
AND HUMBLED HEART, GOD.

PSALM 51:17

A PRAYER FOR JUSTICE TO PREVAIL OVER EVIL

PSALM

For the choir director: with stringed instruments. A Maskil of David.

1 God, listen to my prayer
and do not hide from my plea for help.
2 Pay attention to me and answer me.
I am restless and in turmoil with
my complaint,
3 because of the enemy's words,
because of the pressure of the wicked.
For they bring down disaster on me
and harass me in anger.

4 My heart shudders within me;
terrors of death sweep over me.
5 Fear and trembling grip me;
horror has overwhelmed me.
6 I said, "If only I had wings like a dove!
I would fly away and find rest.
7 How far away I would flee;
I would stay in the wilderness.   *Selah*
8 I would hurry to my shelter
from the raging wind and the storm."

9 Lord, confuse and confound their speech,
for I see violence and strife in the city;
10 day and night they make the rounds on
its walls.
Crime and trouble are within it;

11 destruction is inside it;
oppression and deceit never leave
its marketplace.

12 Now it is not an enemy who insults me—
otherwise I could bear it;
it is not a foe who rises up against me—
otherwise I could hide from him.
13 But it is you, a man who is my peer,
my companion and good friend!
14 We used to have close fellowship;
we walked with the crowd into the
house of God.

15 Let death take them by surprise;
let them go down to Sheol alive,
because evil is in their homes and
within them.
16 But I call to God,
and the LORD will save me.
17 I complain and groan morning, noon,
and night,
and he hears my voice.
18 Though many are against me,
he will redeem me from my battle
unharmed.

19 God, the one enthroned from long ago,
will hear and will humiliate them   *Selah*
because they do not change
and do not fear God.

20 My friend acts violently
against those at peace with him;
he violates his covenant.
21 His buttery words are smooth,
but war is in his heart.
His words are softer than oil,
but they are drawn swords.

22 Cast your burden on the LORD,
and he will sustain you;
he will never allow the righteous to
be shaken.

23 God, you will bring them down
to the Pit of destruction;
men of bloodshed and treachery
will not live out half their days.
But I will trust in you.

AUTHOR ☐ ASAPH ☐ DAVID ☐ SONS OF KORAH ☐ UNSPECIFIED

What emotions are
present in this psalm?

What does the psalm say about the psalmist's circumstance?

☐ ANGER

☐ ANXIETY

☐ DELIGHT

How does the psalmist describe himself?

☐ FEAR

☐ GRATITUDE

☐ GRIEF

☐ HOPE

☐ JOY

What requests are made to God?	What instructions are given to the reader?	How is God addressed and/or described?

☐ LONGING

☐ LOVE

☐ OPTIMISM

☐ PEACE

☐ REMORSE

☐ SORROW

☐ SYMPATHY

☐ OTHER

*For more options, see the "Emotion
in the Psalms" chart on p. 88.*

What situation in my life does this psalm call to mind?

Write your own prayer below.

ADDRESS. DESCRIBE. CONFESS. REQUEST. PRAISE.

BUT I CALL TO GOD,
AND THE LORD WILL SAVE ME.

PSALM 55:16

Use today to pray, rest, and reflect
on this week's reading, giving thanks
for the grace that is ours in Christ.

THIS IS THE CONFIDENCE WE HAVE
BEFORE HIM: IF WE ASK ANYTHING
ACCORDING TO HIS WILL, HE HEARS
US. AND IF WE KNOW THAT HE HEARS
WHATEVER WE ASK, WE KNOW THAT WE
HAVE WHAT WE HAVE ASKED OF HIM.

1 JOHN 5:14-15

GRACE DAY

Scripture is God-breathed and true.
When we memorize it, we carry the
gospel with us wherever we go.

This week's verse reminds us of
God's kindness, mercy, and love.

Find the corresponding memory card
in the back of your book.

FOR YOU, LORD, ARE KIND
AND READY TO FORGIVE,
ABOUNDING IN FAITHFUL LOVE
TO ALL WHO CALL ON YOU.

PSALM 86:5

WEEKLY TRUTH

"I never know a thing well,
till it is burned into
my heart by prayer."

JOHN BUNYAN

A PRAYER FOR GUIDANCE

PSALM

A psalm of David.

1   LORD, hear my prayer.
    In your faithfulness listen to my plea,
    and in your righteousness answer me.
2   Do not bring your servant into judgment,
    for no one alive is righteous in your sight.

3   For the enemy has pursued me,
    crushing me to the ground,
    making me live in darkness
    like those long dead.
4   My spirit is weak within me;
    my heart is overcome with dismay.

5   I remember the days of old;
    I meditate on all you have done;
    I reflect on the work of your hands.
6   I spread out my hands to you;
    I am like parched land before you.   *Selah*

7   Answer me quickly, LORD;
    my spirit fails.

Don't hide your face from me,
or I will be like those
going down to the Pit.
8   Let me experience
your faithful love in the morning,
for I trust in you.
Reveal to me the way I should go
because I appeal to you.
9   Rescue me from my enemies, LORD;
I come to you for protection.
10 Teach me to do your will,
for you are my God.
May your gracious Spirit
lead me on level ground.

11 For your name's sake, LORD,
let me live.
In your righteousness deliver me from trouble,
12 and in your faithful love destroy my enemies.
Wipe out all those who attack me,
for I am your servant.

AUTHOR   ☐ ASAPH   ☐ DAVID   ☐ SONS OF KORAH   ☐ UNSPECIFIED

What emotions are present in this psalm?

What does the psalm say about the psalmist's circumstance?

☐ ANGER

☐ ANXIETY

☐ DELIGHT

☐ FEAR

How does the psalmist describe himself?

☐ GRATITUDE

☐ GRIEF

☐ HOPE

☐ JOY

What requests are made to God?	What instructions are given to the reader?	How is God addressed and/or described?

☐ LONGING

☐ LOVE

☐ OPTIMISM

☐ PEACE

☐ REMORSE

☐ SORROW

☐ SYMPATHY

☐ OTHER

For more options, see the "Emotion in the Psalms" chart on p. 88.

What situation in my life does this psalm call to mind?

Write your own prayer below.

ADDRESS. DESCRIBE. CONFESS. REQUEST. PRAISE.

REVEAL TO ME THE WAY
I SHOULD GO BECAUSE
I APPEAL TO YOU.

PSALM 143:8

A PRAYER FOR HELP IN TROUBLE

PSALM

A Maskil of David. When he was in the cave. A prayer.

1   I cry aloud to the Lord;
    I plead aloud to the Lord for mercy.
2   I pour out my complaint before him;
    I reveal my trouble to him.
3   Although my spirit is weak within me,
    you know my way.

    Along this path I travel
    they have hidden a trap for me.
4   Look to the right and see:
    no one stands up for me;
    there is no refuge for me;
    no one cares about me.

5   I cry to you, Lord;
    I say, "You are my shelter,
    my portion in the land of the living."
6   Listen to my cry,
    for I am very weak.
    Rescue me from those who pursue me,
    for they are too strong for me.
7   Free me from prison
    so that I can praise your name.
    The righteous will gather around me
    because you deal generously with me.

AUTHOR   ☐ ASAPH   ☐ DAVID   ☐ SONS OF KORAH   ☐ UNSPECIFIED

What emotions are present in this psalm?

What does the psalm say about the psalmist's circumstance?

☐ ANGER

☐ ANXIETY

☐ DELIGHT

☐ FEAR

How does the psalmist describe himself?

☐ GRATITUDE

☐ GRIEF

☐ HOPE

☐ JOY

What requests are made to God?	What instructions are given to the reader?	How is God addressed and/or described?

☐ LONGING

☐ LOVE

☐ OPTIMISM

☐ PEACE

☐ REMORSE

☐ SORROW

☐ SYMPATHY

☐ OTHER

For more options, see the "Emotion in the Psalms" chart on p. 88.

What situation in my life does this psalm call to mind?

Write your own prayer below.

ADDRESS. DESCRIBE. CONFESS. REQUEST. PRAISE.

RESCUE ME FROM THOSE WHO PURSUE ME,
FOR THEY ARE TOO STRONG FOR ME.

PSALM 142:6

The book of Psalms is filled with expressions of human emotion. God gave us emotions, and it is important that we are able to express a range of feelings when we pray. Here are some of the emotions found in the book of Psalms, arranged by category.

SADNESS 30:5

_____

JOY 4:7

_____

LOVE 18:1

_____

ANGER 74:11

_____

FEAR 55:4-8

_____

SURPRISE 55:15-16

_____

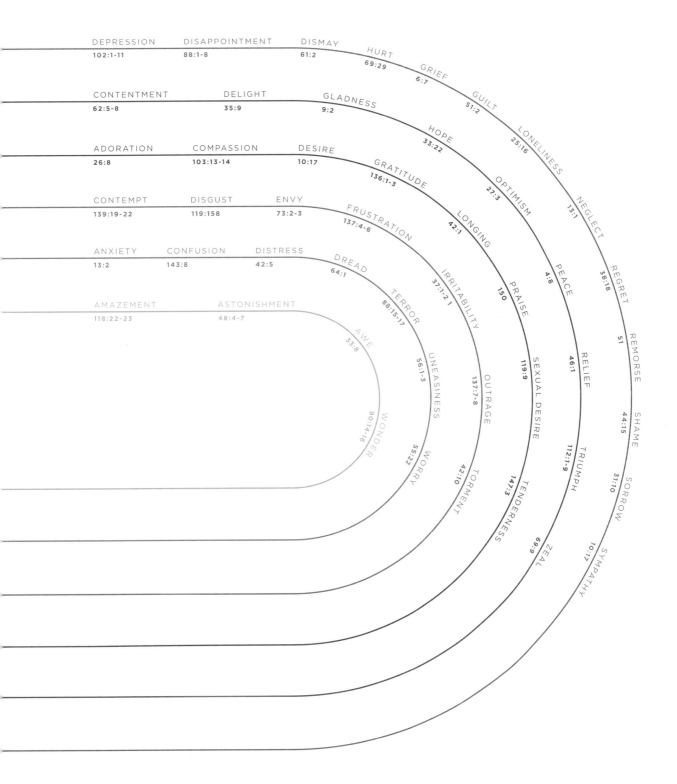

DEPRESSION 102:1-11　DISAPPOINTMENT 88:1-8　DISMAY 61:2　HURT 69:29　GRIEF 6:7　GUILT 51:2　LONELINESS 25:16　NEGLECT 13:1　REGRET 38:18　REMORSE 51　SHAME 44:15　SORROW 31:10　SYMPATHY 10:17

CONTENTMENT 62:5-8　DELIGHT 35:9　GLADNESS 9:2　HOPE 33:22　OPTIMISM 27:3　PEACE 4:8　RELIEF 46:1　TRIUMPH 112:1-9　ZEAL 69:9

ADORATION 26:8　COMPASSION 103:13-14　DESIRE 10:17　GRATITUDE 136:1-3　LONGING 42:1　PRAISE 150　SEXUAL DESIRE 119:9　TENDERNESS 147:3

CONTEMPT 139:19-22　DISGUST 119:158　ENVY 73:2-3　FRUSTRATION 137:4-6　IRRITABILITY 37:1-2 1　OUTRAGE 137:7-8　TORMENT 42:10

ANXIETY 13:2　CONFUSION 143:8　DISTRESS 42:5　DREAD 64:1　TERROR 88:15-17　UNEASINESS 56:1-3　WORRY 55:22

AMAZEMENT 118:22-23　ASTONISHMENT 48:4-7　AWE 33:8　WONDER 90:14-16

A PRAYER OF ADORATION

PSALM

¹ Hallelujah!
My soul, praise the LORD.
² I will praise the LORD all my life;
I will sing to my God as long as I live.

³ Do not trust in nobles,
in a son of man, who cannot save.
⁴ When his breath leaves him,
he returns to the ground;
on that day his plans die.

⁵ Happy is the one whose help is the God
of Jacob,
whose hope is in the LORD his God,
⁶ the Maker of heaven and earth,
the sea and everything in them.
He remains faithful forever,
⁷ executing justice for the exploited
and giving food to the hungry.
The LORD frees prisoners.
⁸ The LORD opens the eyes of the blind.
The LORD raises up those who are oppressed.
The LORD loves the righteous.
⁹ The LORD protects resident aliens
and helps the fatherless and the widow,
but he frustrates the ways of the wicked.

¹⁰ The LORD reigns forever;
Zion, your God reigns for all generations.
Hallelujah!

AUTHOR ☐ ASAPH ☐ DAVID ☐ SONS OF KORAH ☐ UNSPECIFIED

What emotions are present in this psalm?

What does the psalm say about the psalmist's circumstance?

☐ ANGER

☐ ANXIETY

☐ DELIGHT

How does the psalmist describe himself?

☐ FEAR

☐ GRATITUDE

☐ GRIEF

☐ HOPE

☐ JOY

What requests are made to God?	What instructions are given to the reader?	How is God addressed and/or described?

☐ LONGING

☐ LOVE

☐ OPTIMISM

☐ PEACE

☐ REMORSE

☐ SORROW

☐ SYMPATHY

☐ OTHER

_____

For more options, see the "Emotion in the Psalms" chart on p. 88.

What situation in my life does this psalm call to mind?

Write your own prayer below.

ADDRESS. DESCRIBE. CONFESS. REQUEST. PRAISE.

HE REMAINS FAITHFUL FOREVER

PSALM 146:6

A PRAYER FOR THE CHURCH

PSALM

For the choir director: on the Gittith. A psalm of the sons of Korah.

1 How lovely is your dwelling place,
Lord of Armies.

2 I long and yearn
for the courts of the Lord;
my heart and flesh cry out for the living God.

3 Even a sparrow finds a home,
and a swallow, a nest for herself
where she places her young—
near your altars, Lord of Armies,
my King and my God.

4 How happy are those who reside in your house,
who praise you continually.   *Selah*

5 Happy are the people whose strength is in you,
whose hearts are set on pilgrimage.

6 As they pass through the Valley of Baca,
they make it a source of springwater;
even the autumn rain will cover it with
blessings.

7 They go from strength to strength;
each appears before God in Zion.

8 Lord God of Armies, hear my prayer;
listen, God of Jacob.   *Selah*

9 Consider our shield, God;
look on the face of your anointed one.

10 Better a day in your courts
than a thousand anywhere else.
I would rather stand at the threshold
of the house of my God
than live in the tents of wicked people.

11 For the Lord God is a sun and shield.
The Lord grants favor and honor;
he does not withhold the good
from those who live with integrity.

12 Happy is the person who trusts in you,
Lord of Armies!

AUTHOR   ☐ ASAPH   ☐ DAVID   ☐ SONS OF KORAH   ☐ UNSPECIFIED

What emotions are
present in this psalm?

What does the psalm say about the psalmist's circumstance?

☐ ANGER

☐ ANXIETY

☐ DELIGHT

☐ FEAR

How does the psalmist describe himself?

☐ GRATITUDE

☐ GRIEF

☐ HOPE

☐ JOY

What requests are made to God? | What instructions are given to the reader? | How is God addressed and/or described?

☐ LONGING

☐ LOVE

☐ OPTIMISM

☐ PEACE

☐ REMORSE

☐ SORROW

☐ SYMPATHY

☐ OTHER

For more options, see the "Emotion in the Psalms" chart on p. 88.

What situation in my life does this psalm call to mind?

Write your own prayer below.

ADDRESS. DESCRIBE. CONFESS. REQUEST. PRAISE.

BETTER A DAY IN YOUR
COURTS THAN A THOUSAND
ANYWHERE ELSE.

PSALM 84:10

A PRAYER CELEBRATING THE GIFT OF JESUS

PSALM

1 Why do the nations rage
  and the peoples plot in vain?
2 The kings of the earth take their stand,
  and the rulers conspire together
  against the LORD and his Anointed One:
3 "Let's tear off their chains
  and throw their ropes off of us."

4 The one enthroned in heaven laughs;
  the Lord ridicules them.
5 Then he speaks to them in his anger
  and terrifies them in his wrath:
6 "I have installed my king
  on Zion, my holy mountain."

7 I will declare the LORD's decree.
  He said to me, "You are my Son;
  today I have become your Father.
8 Ask of me,
  and I will make the nations your inheritance
  and the ends of the earth your possession.
9 You will break them with an iron scepter;
  you will shatter them like pottery."

10 So now, kings, be wise;
   receive instruction, you judges of the earth.
11 Serve the LORD with reverential awe
   and rejoice with trembling.
12 Pay homage to the Son or he will be angry
   and you will perish in your rebellion,
   for his anger may ignite at any moment.
   All who take refuge in him are happy.

AUTHOR ☐ ASAPH ☐ DAVID ☐ SONS OF KORAH ☐ UNSPECIFIED

| What emotions are present in this psalm? | What does the psalm say about the psalmist's circumstance? |

☐ ANGER

☐ ANXIETY

☐ DELIGHT

☐ FEAR

How does the psalmist describe himself?

☐ GRATITUDE

☐ GRIEF

☐ HOPE

☐ JOY

What requests are made to God?	What instructions are given to the reader?	How is God addressed and/or described?

☐ LONGING

☐ LOVE

☐ OPTIMISM

☐ PEACE

☐ REMORSE

☐ SORROW

☐ SYMPATHY

☐ OTHER

For more options, see the "Emotion in the Psalms" chart on p. 88.

What situation in my life does this psalm call to mind?

Write your own prayer below.

ADDRESS. DESCRIBE. CONFESS. REQUEST. PRAISE.

SERVE THE LORD WITH
REVERENTIAL AWE
AND REJOICE WITH
TREMBLING.

PSALM 2:11

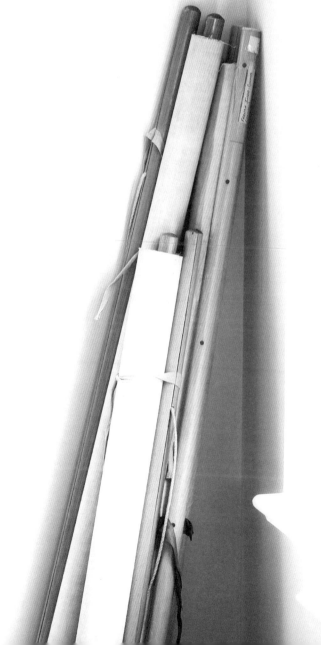

Use today to pray, rest, and reflect
on this week's reading, giving thanks
for the grace that is ours in Christ.

DON'T WORRY ABOUT ANYTHING,
BUT IN EVERYTHING, THROUGH PRAYER
AND PETITION WITH THANKSGIVING,
PRESENT YOUR REQUESTS TO GOD.
AND THE PEACE OF GOD, WHICH SURPASSES
ALL UNDERSTANDING, WILL GUARD YOUR
HEARTS AND MINDS IN CHRIST JESUS.

PHILIPPIANS 4:6-7

GRACE DAY

Scripture is God-breathed and true.
When we memorize it, we carry the
gospel with us wherever we go.

This week's verse reminds us to go
to God first when we need help.

Find the corresponding memory card
in the back of your book.

LET ME EXPERIENCE
YOUR FAITHFUL LOVE IN THE MORNING,
FOR I TRUST IN YOU.
REVEAL TO ME THE WAY I SHOULD GO
BECAUSE I APPEAL TO YOU.

PSALM 143:8

WEEKLY TRUTH

"Prayer is my chief work,
and it is by means of it
that I carry on the rest."

THOMAS HOOKER

MATERIALS

Craft Smart® Black Broad Tip
Chalk Marker

Tracing paper

TIPS

Dry brush lettering is meant to be a casual, imperfect script.
Don't worry about following the guide exactly.

A chalk marker, normally meant for mirrors and glass, is a
great tool for achieving a dry-brushed look without wearing
down a marker or using brushes and paint.

Make your strokes somewhat quickly to make the letters
flow, touching the pen lightly to the paper as you write.

Practice writing on different papers. Vellum tracing paper
will give each letter a smoother finish, while standard
printer paper will have a drier look.

EXPERIMENT WITH HOLDING THE MARKER AT DIFFERENT
ANGLES TO GET VARYING WIDTHS AND TEXTURES.

Aa Bb Cc Dd Ee

Ff Gg Hh Ii Jj

Kk Ll Mm Nn

Oo Pp Qq Rr Ss

Tt Uu Vv Ww

Xx Yy Zz

DOWNLOAD THE APP

STOP BY
shereadstruth.com

SHOP
shopshereadstruth.com

SEND A NOTE
hello@shereadstruth.com

CONNECT
#SheReadsTruth

SHE READS TRUTH *is a worldwide community of women who read God's Word together every day.*

Founded in 2012, She Reads Truth invites women of all ages to engage with Scripture through daily reading plans, online conversation led by a vibrant community of contributors, and offline resources created at the intersection of beauty, goodness, and Truth.

WHERE DID I STUDY?

O HOME
O OFFICE
O COFFEE SHOP
O CHURCH
O A FRIEND'S HOUSE
O OTHER

WHAT WAS I LISTENING TO?

ARTIST:

SONG:

PLAYLIST:

WHEN DID I STUDY?

MORNING
AFTERNOON
NIGHT

My closing prayer:

WHAT WAS HAPPENING IN MY LIFE?

WHAT WAS HAPPENING IN THE WORLD?

| MONTH | DAY | YEAR |

END DATE